Ten Teachings from Paul's Letters

by Philip and
Randi Quanbeck

Bible Basics for Adults

Augsburg Fortress, Minneapolis

Contents

1 **BELONGING AS ONE IN CHRIST**   3
   The Big Picture (1 Corinthians 12:12-26)
   One In Christ (Ephesians 2:19-22)

2 **A NEW LIFE IN CHRIST**   11
   Dying and Rising with Christ (Romans 6:1-5)
   The Lord's Supper: "For You" (1 Corinthians 11:23-26)

3 **PAUL'S BOLDNESS IN PREACHING**   19
   There Is No Other Gospel (Galatians 1:10-12)
   Christ: The Power and Wisdom of God (1 Cor. 1:18-25; 2:1-5)

4 **THE FREEDOM OF THE CHRISTIAN**   31
   Life In the Spirit (Romans 8:1-4)
   Christian Freedom (Galatians 5:13-14)

5 **GOD AS PROVIDER**   39
   God's Comfort (2 Corinthians 1:3-4)
   God's Promise (Romans 1:1-4)

6 **REJOICE IN THE LORD ALWAYS**   46
   No Need for Anxiety (Philippians 4:4-7)

   BIBLE HELPS   23-26
   GLOSSARY   Inside back cover

BIBLE BASICS FOR ADULTS
Ten Key Teachings from Paul's Letters Learner Book
This learner book has a corresponding leader guide.

Editors: Katherine A. Evensen and Rich Gordon
Designer: Craig P. Claeys. Illustrators: Mari Goering, Judy Swanson
Cover photo: © Lars Hansen Photography

Unless otherwise noted, scripture quotations are from New Revised Standard Version Bible, copyright 1989 Division of Christian Education of the National Council of the Churches of Christ in the United States of America. Used by permission. Scripture quotations marked TEV are from Today's English Version of the Bible, Second Edition, copyright © 1992 by the American Bible Society. Used by permission. Scripture quotations marked NIV are from The Holy Bible, New International Version®. Copyright © 1973, 1978, 1984 by International Bible Society. Used by permission of Zondervan Publishing House. All rights reserved. The "NIV" and "New International Version" trademarks are registered in the United States Patent and Trademark Office by International Bible Society. Use of either trademark requires the permission of International Bible Society.

Copyright © 1998 Augsburg Fortress
All rights reserved. May not be reproduced.

ISBN 0-8066-3634-3

Manufactured in U.S.A.
1 2 3 4 5 6 7 8 9 0 1 2 3 4 5 6 7 8 9

1 Belonging as One in Christ

The church, through its many members, is but one body.

1 Corinthians 12:12-26   The Big Picture

IN A COMPETITIVE WORLD, most of us are pretty conscious of who has the power and who doesn't, as well as those who abuse power by demeaning others. The use and abuse of power and position is a basic issue for the human community. Paul knows that division is the result of a power struggle and that words reflecting strong feelings and division in the church must be addressed head-on rather than ignored. It may seem that Paul minimizes the struggle by using the example of the human body to create a paradigm for the church.

But when Paul uses the example of the human body, he is not trying to be simplistic or put a sentimental face on the division that is caused by the power of sin. He is taking the issue very seriously but tries to remind us of the "big picture"—namely, the entire community in Christ.

The glue that holds everything together, says Paul, is our baptism. Through baptism, God has taken the initiative in shaping the Christian community and the church. Baptism is where it all begins because that is where the healing starts. No matter how severe the separation, in our baptism we are liberated both from our own unreasonable demands and from trying to save ourselves by the world's standards. Baptism gives us another model for living that is radically different from the world in which we live.

Baptism, through water and the word, is the way God creates a new community in Christ where power struggles or distinctions cannot make any difference. The old divisions based on rank, intelligence, talent, success, material possessions, class, looks, and even personality cannot apply in the church. Baptism initiates a new beginning for us. Baptism is a break from the past, a radical break from our former selves. In baptism, God makes us "new creations" (2 Corinthians 5:17). In our baptism God places us on an equal footing with all other Christians—past, present, and future. We are united with Christ so that our life no longer belongs to us but to Christ.

> **Therefore we have been buried with him by baptism into death, so that, just as Christ was raised from the dead by the glory of the Father, so we too might walk in newness of life.**
>
> Romans 6:4

Through baptism and the word of Christ that heals and makes us whole, terrible and strong divisions can be healed and overcome. Paul is convinced of the power of Christ through baptism to make things right and to set the church on a path of rejoicing. In one of Charles Schulz's "Peanuts" comic strips, Snoopy is shown dancing on his toes, smiling radiantly and saying, "I'm so glad I'm a Christian, I could just dance!" But the next frame shows a serious Snoopy with the comment, "But then I'd get kicked out of the church."

Baptism defies that kind of thinking. Baptism is such an act of liberation that to realize our new freedom might well set us to dancing. Maybe our dance will be to feed the hungry or clothe the naked. Maybe our dance will be intercessory prayer. Maybe our dance will propel us into realms of caring we might have never envisioned. Regardless of what steps we take, our dance will be a dance of joy. Even when we listen to the hurting, we will do so out of a sense of privilege rather than duty, so radical is the nature of our baptism.

Sometimes it's difficult to think of the entire church suffering when one part suffers, or rejoicing when one part rejoices. Paul contends that when we are baptized into the body of Christ, something of our personal identity is lost for the sake of the whole. However, because Paul knew that Christ is there for us in the midst of the church, working healing and renewal, that such a loss of personal identity is insignificant.

> **Paul's Vocation (Acts 18:3)**
> Paul was a tentmaker, we think. The reference to Paul working with his hands is in Acts 18:3, where it says they were of the same trade—tentmakers.

Through this Christian community, Christ works his salvation. That is why baptism in Christ is the starting point for the church, and it is also where it returns every day to get the "big picture."

Ephesians 2:19-22   One In Christ

DIVISION BETWEEN Jewish and Gentile (non-Jewish) Christians is the background for this text. Paul is making this statement in light of the Jewish community's claim to being the chosen people of God because of its identity and heritage. The temple in Jerusalem was a key element in forming Jewish identity, so Paul uses the analogy of bricks and mortar to establish the credibility of the Gentile Christian community. No longer "foreigner and aliens," the Gentiles are called to be "fellow citizens of God's household," with Christ as the cornerstone. This means that the Gentiles have all the same rights and privileges in the church as their Jewish counterparts.

> **Many scholars** regard Paul's letter to the Ephesians as a "circular" letter that was distributed to churches throughout Asia Minor.

When Paul talks about the church, he is constructing a new view of what it means to belong to the church community as Jew or Gentile. The Spirit of Christ reshapes the entire church structure in a new way, says Paul. The work of the Holy Spirit shapes the new community in Christ.

Until Christ came, the "church" consisted entirely of Jewish people (usually referred to as "Israel"). They were God's chosen people going back to the covenant God made with Abraham (Genesis 17:1-8). The Jewish people remain God's chosen people, for God's promises are forever. But in Christ, Gentiles (non-Jews) were also brought into the church. Paul describes our inclusion into God's family as one of "adoption" (Galatians 4:5). Israel had difficulty believing that any non-Jew could be incorporated into the church, and consequently, many of the struggles within the early church centered around this question of inclusivity.

> **Paul's letter** to the Ephesians centers around the idea that the church has been called by God, redeemed and forgiven through Jesus, and incorporated into a community by the Holy Spirit. This threefold aspect of understanding God is called Trinitarian, sometimes referred to as three-in-one.

When Paul uses the term *household*, he means that we have a Father in whose house we belong as family members. To be a member of a family isn't always tranquil. Often, family members fight and there are problems to overcome. But Jesus is the "chief cornerstone" in which the whole building is "joined together and grows into a holy temple in the Lord" (Ephesians 2:21). What used to be just a building made of ordinary materials has now become a holy place. Of course, what needs to be remembered is that the cornerstone is rejected (Psalm 118:22). Christ is crucified. The cross looms before us and its shadow covers all. The Holy Spirit comes to enlighten our minds and renew our spirits. God's will shall reign despite whatever obstacles lie before it.

> **But Jesus is the "chief cornerstone" in which the whole building is "joined together and grows into a holy temple in the Lord."**
> Ephesians 2:21

Jesus creates the church from dust and ashes, from the ruins of the old Jewish order, and infuses it with new life. All of the old barriers to community are broken and a new bond is made—the bond of the Spirit. Paul wants us to understand that the limitations of the old order are not strong enough to contain the Spirit of Christ. Now, a new structure is built that rests upon the old.

As a Christian community, we inherit the work of the apostles and prophets, but we cannot define ourselves entirely by their work. We inherit the legacy of the Jewish people, and that history is part of the foundation of the new church. Christ has laid a new foundation and is the cornerstone of a new church. That is where the hope and redemption and vitality of a new church are for us today.

In this passage Paul uses the old examples of community to bridge the transition to the new community in Christ. With his words, Paul makes possible the transition of a community that divides on the basis of all kinds of criteria to one that unites on the basis of the Spirit of Christ alone. Without anything other than the promise of the Spirit, the church is called into existence. Paul's radically transforming message is one we should not forget, namely, the church does not necessarily have to be "one" to be faithful to its calling. It simply has to be one "in Christ."

> **Paul uses** a similar greeting and ending in each of his letters. They typically start with "Paul, called to be an apostle of Christ Jesus," or "Paul, an apostle of Christ Jesus by the will of God." They end with "The grace of our Lord Jesus Christ be with you all."

Belonging as One in Christ

Focus the Stories

One Body, Many Members

Reflect on the following questions:

1. Paul makes an analogy between the church and our physical body. How does that make it easier for us to understand the value of each person in our congregation?

2. We know that when one of our family members is hurt, we hurt, too. Paul writes of the church, "If one member suffers, all suffer together with it; if one member is honored, all rejoice together with it" (1 Corinthians 12:26). What does this statement tell us about our relationship to one another in the body of Christ?

3. Being a stranger (much less an alien!) is an uncomfortable situation. But the early Christians felt themselves to be just that among the Old Testament believers. How might you react in that situation to Paul's declaration: "So then you are no longer strangers and aliens, but you are citizens with the saints and also members of the household of God" (Ephesians 2:19)? How would you describe "citizenship with the saints and the household of God?"

4. In architecture, the cornerstone is a vital part of any construction. Without it, the lines of a building may become grossly out of proportion to its original dimensions. So what is Paul implying when he calls Jesus the "cornerstone...in whom the whole structure is joined together"? What are the "cornerstones" in your life?

5. What are the essential qualities a church must have for you to want to be part of its membership? What aspects of congregational life "turn you off?"

Essential qualities a chuch must have:

Aspects of congregational life that "turn me off":

Closing

God has shaped our community into one body where we exist as equals and acknowledge our interdependence upon one another, recognizing that whatever affects anyone in the body of Christ affects the rest of us as well. The Spirit of Christ has restructured the church so that any division that exists in the church cannot be tolerated. We are simply one in Christ!

Closing prayer: God, in our Baptism you have made us one people. Thank you for including us in your family and making us brothers and sisters to all humanity. Give us hearts open to your love that we might be so filled with the joy of acceptance, that we will form circles of love that include everyone. Amen.

2. A New Life in Christ

We have been set free through Jesus Christ.

Romans 6:1-5 Dying and Rising with Christ

WHAT SHALL WE SAY, THEN? Shall we go on sinning so that grace may increase?" (Romans 6:1 NIV). There is an attractive logic in this statement. As Christians, we profess to believe that sin comes naturally. The secular world has trouble with such a belief, believing instead that the world runs on the basis of a logical order of cause and effect. Everything starts from some explainable, tangible point and has a good reason for working the way it does.

Paul says no to the equation of cause and effect, namely that more sin equals more grace. We are going to sin no matter how hard we try not to, because we can't change what Paul believes is our basic sinful nature. Left to ourselves, we will fall prey to passions and desires that we can't control, even with logic and good intentions.

Paul says that the world's order of cause and effect does not work in the life and death struggle for the Christian. How can we possibly reconcile our love of sin and life to the love of Christ? In our baptism, Jesus is the power that transforms us from "slaves of sin" to being "freed from sin" because the power of Jesus' love is greater than the power of sin.

Paul is not giving us "pie in the sky," but rather a concrete proposal: "We were therefore buried with him through baptism into death in order that, just as Christ was raised from the dead through the glory of the Father, we too may live a new life" (Romans 6:4 NIV). This is not the order of cause and effect, but the order of a new relationship that is stronger than cause and effect.

Paul says that "if we have been united with him like this in his death, we will certainly also be united with him in his resurrection" (Romans 6:5 NIV), though it is not clear how and when this should be. At what point are we resurrected after death? That debate has been around since the New Testament was written. Some Bible scholars believe our resurrection takes place at the time of our death, citing Jesus' promise to the thief who was crucified at the same time as Jesus. "Truly I tell you," Jesus asserted, "today you will be with me in Paradise" (Luke 23:43). Other Bible scholars contend that at the time of our death we enter a deep sleep and our resurrection is delayed until the end times when Jesus comes again. They use Paul's first letter to the Thessalonians (4:16-17) to support their view. The relationship that centers on the cross and resurrection is first and foremost union with Christ.

What do we say, then? We say that we are dead to sin and that it no longer has the last word for our lives. Sin "shall not be your master, because you are... under grace" (Romans 6:14 NIV). Simply stated, grace is the undeserved goodness of God. God's love for us is so profound and abundant it defies our ability to comprehend such favor. Just to be able to realize that we are under grace may be the simplest word of hope for those who are perishing under the weight of guilt, despair, loneliness, depression, anger, ignorance, denial, and self-hatred. Every psychological category imaginable can be included in this passage. Perhaps the most dangerous category of all is the one that says we have no sin. Christ promises us that Christ's death on the cross was for us so that we might live with him and

> **Paul uses** a cause and effect debating style to illustrate a theology that is anything but cause and effect! Paul's use of "if–then" rhetorical style in his writing is shown in this passage in Romans 6:5 (NIV): "If we have been united with him like this in his death, (then) we will certainly also be united with him in his resur-rection." And again in Romans 6:8 (NIV): "Now if we died with Christ, (then) we believe that we will also live with him."

find life in abundance. The life that Jesus gives is a life of grace. In our baptism God gives evidence of grace by claiming us to be God's children. We can bring nothing to our baptism besides ourselves. We can give nothing but to yield our will to God. We can do nothing but submit. Baptism is God's act of grace.

We arise from that event a new creation. Our old selves have been cast aside like a useless cocoon. Washed clean, we arise and "walk in newness of life" (Romans 6:4) to begin a resurrection of our life in the Spirit. We are changed. Made new. Cleansed. Welcomed into the family of God.

At this time we enter a dual existence. We are freed from sin, yet remain in bondage to sin. "How can this be?" we ask. Martin Luther explained this dual existence by using the word *simultaneous*. We are "simultaneously" saint and sinner. We are sinners because we have a propensity to sin. That is what we are.

But we have been washed clean in our baptism. Jesus' robe of righteousness covers us and our sinfulness in a blanket of grace. The power of sin to separate us from God has been destroyed by Christ Jesus, so while we continue to think and act in sinful ways, the love of Christ prevents our separation from God.

> ***For sin will have no dominion over you, since you are not under law but under grace.***
>
> Romans 6:14

A New Life in Christ   13

1 Corinthians 11:23-26
The Lord's Supper: "For You"

"THE BODY OF CHRIST...given for you."
"The blood of Christ...shed for you."
For you. These words of life ring in our ears and sing in our hearts. For me? The body of Christ. The blood of Christ. For me? "Is it really so?" we ask, daring to believe what is so difficult to comprehend. *For you* is the response from God.

It is not easy to trust that when God says *for you* in the Lord's Supper that God has done enough for us. Comprehending the depth of God's love for us is a lifetime task we may never finish.

The words *for you* mean that Jesus' life and death were for the purpose of giving life to the world beyond anyone's wildest dreams. It is the "for you" of the lover who holds out a hand offering love in all its vulnerability. It is putting oneself in harm's way for the love of another, even if it means sacrificing one's own life as Jesus did for us.

But Jesus is not a hero. Jesus is a savior, the embodiment of God's new covenant. Paul talks about the "new covenant" that is given in the Lord's Supper. This covenant is a promise that God will be with us and will work for our salvation through the church in the human community.

> **But this is the covenant that I will make with the house of Israel after those days, says the LORD: I will put my law within them, and I will write it on their hearts; and I will be their God, and they shall be my people. No longer shall they teach one another, or say to each other, "Know the LORD," for they shall all know me, from the least of them to the greatest, says the LORD; for I will forgive their iniquity, and remember their sin no more.**
>
> Jeremiah 31:33-34

The old covenant is the Ten Commandments and the law. It tells us that we have not acted the way we should have. The old covenant convicts us of our sin in no uncertain terms. There is no grace, no freedom, no advocate for us. The law shows us our sin and gives us no way to appeal. We are guilty, and we must pay the penalty. To try to live by the letter of the law is to try to do the impossible. In short, we are driven to despair and to the gates of hell because we can't meet its demands on us.

> **A covenant** is an agreement. Some covenants are unilateral, as the verses from Jeremiah indicate. God is acting alone. Some covenants require action by two or more parties: "Then you shall call, and the LORD will answer; you shall cry for help, and he will say, Here I am" (Isaiah 58:9).

The good news is that Jesus is the new covenant. Jesus is our advocate and defense lawyer just as the drama of the courtroom and the law is starting. Jesus takes our place on the witness stand and pleads for our defense as well. He is both judge and jury ruling in our favor. Christ takes on the entire law and overturns the verdict. He breaks the chains that have kept us trying to meet every legal expectation of the old covenant and tells us we can go free. This is what it means to "do this in remembrance of me." When we receive the Lord's Supper, we are part of the new covenant—a new drama that sets us free from the law and the penalty of death. It is the gospel of our Lord!

Jesus says we do not need to fear the outcome of our lives because in Christ and Christ's new covenant, our sins are covered. The bill is paid, and all we need to do is "proclaim the Lord's death until he comes."

What it means to "proclaim the Lord's death" is to live a new and different kind of life in the community of Christ, a life of one who has been set free. Christ tells us that our participation in remembering Christ's death and resurrection means that we proclaim Christ's death "until (Jesus) comes." We can enjoy the privilege of bringing the good news of the new covenant to those who need to hear a message of good news.

Focus the Stories

Psalm 13 (NIV)

How long, O LORD? Will you forget me forever?
    How long will you hide your face from me?
How long must I wrestle with my thoughts
    and every day have sorrow in my heart?
    How long will my enemy triumph over me?
Look on me and answer, O LORD my God.
    Give light to my eyes, or I will sleep in death;
my enemy will say, "I have overcome him,"
    and my foes will rejoice when I fall.
But I trust in your unfailing love;
    my heart rejoices in your salvation.
I will sing to the LORD,
    for he has been good to me.

1. Have you ever felt as hopeless as the Psalmist does in the first few verses of Psalm 13? Yet by the end of the Psalm the writer's heart is filled with hope. How did that happen? Does Paul ever reflect an attitude of hopelessness? How do you cope with a feeling of hopelessness?

2. How can we trust God in the words *for you*? What is the difference between knowing something is "for you" and believing something is "for you"? Does faith depend on trust?

3. "…in remembrance of me." How do we remember those we love? What helps us to think of times worth remembering? What kinds of impressions are important? Is simply remembering enough? What goes beyond remembering?

4. Have you ever been imprisoned by a habit, an old way of thinking, a compulsion, or by outside forces? How did your freedom take place? How were you affected by your release? What does it mean to be set free? Why do we desire to proclaim our freedom?

5. Think about the idea of having faith in something or someone. What goes into having faith? Where does any kind of faith come from? Are there other words for faith that you can think of, such as *confidence, reliability,* and *proof*? Where do we get our ideas for faith? Is "leap" of faith an accurate portrayal of faith?

6. At what point do you think the resurrection of the dead takes place? At the time of death? When Jesus comes again? At another time? What difference does it make to you regarding the time of our resurrection?

Closing

Our sinful nature and sinful ways separate us from God. But no longer! God, in the name of Christ, took the punishment for our sins, changing the whole order of our being so that we are no longer under the mastery of sin but of grace (Romans 6:14). The old covenant that convicted us of our sin is replaced by a new covenant of grace. To help us realize the reality of God's forgiveness, Jesus instituted a holy supper, an expression of grace succinctly stated in two words: *for you.*

Closing prayer: Thank you, Lord Jesus, for setting us free from our sin. Strengthen us in our faith that we may be filled with your peace that passes understanding, your joy that surpasses pleasure, and your love that exceeds expectations. Amen.

3. Paul's Boldness in Preaching

The power and wisdom of God is expressed in the Gospel of Jesus Christ.

Galatians 1:10-12 There Is No Other Gospel

IN PAUL'S DAY, as well as in ours, all kinds of people were continually making claims to be a prophet or even the Messiah. There were street preachers calling out the time of the end of the world, dealers in sorcery and fortunes, and the ever-present astrologers and palm readers. In the Jewish community, the Messiah was still the Expected One who would create order out of chaos and bring the Roman rulers to their knees. We can imagine the church in Galatia falling prey to the external pressures of the culture when Paul begins the letter to the Galatians by expressing his dismay at their lack of constancy (Galatians 1:6).

> *Now before faith came, we were imprisoned and guarded under the law until faith would be revealed. Therefore the law was our disciplinarian until Christ came, so that we might be justified by faith. But now that faith has come, we are no longer subject to a disciplinarian, for in Christ Jesus you are all children of God through faith.*
>
> Galatians 3:23-26

The church in Galatia, consisting mostly of Gentiles, was being gradually occupied by forces that began to crowd out the Gospel of Christ.

Paul knew that the church in Galatia was facing extreme pressures against its very existence. All types of thinking were present in this multicultural area. Could the message of the gospel be heard over this cacophony of voices that threatened to dilute and obscure the central message of the gospel (Christ crucified)?

> *My friends, if anyone is detected in a transgression, you who have received the Spirit should restore such a one in a spirit of gentleness. Take care that you yourselves are not tempted.*
>
> Galatians 6:1

Paul's response to this situation of conflict is hard-hitting and intense. Paul is vehemently opposed to anyone who thinks they can amend, change, improve, or alter in any way the Gospel of Christ by which they were first brought to faith. Paul is making a clear claim for the exclusivity of the Gospel message of Christ, leaving no room for debate (Galatians 1:9).

In Galatians Paul insists that a person becomes right with God only through faith in Christ and not by any ritual observances or good works (Galatians 2:16).

The intensity of Paul's conviction is unmistakable. Paul is certain of his right to preach the Gospel of Christ because he received it directly "by revelation from Jesus Christ" (Galatians 1:12 NIV). This from a man who had formerly persecuted the Christian community with equal intensity.

Paul makes two claims in the beginning of Galatians: first, that his Gospel message is from God alone and revealed by Christ directly, and second, that he has every right in the world to preach it and to insist on its exclusivity and integrity.

What right does Paul have to denigrate and extinguish Jewish law? He obviously knows it by heart, but seems to delight in treading on it whenever possible: "All who rely on observing the law

The word Paul used for "restore" in Galatians 6:1 is a medical term that means, "to set a broken bone."

Ten Key Teachings from Paul's Letters

Paul's World

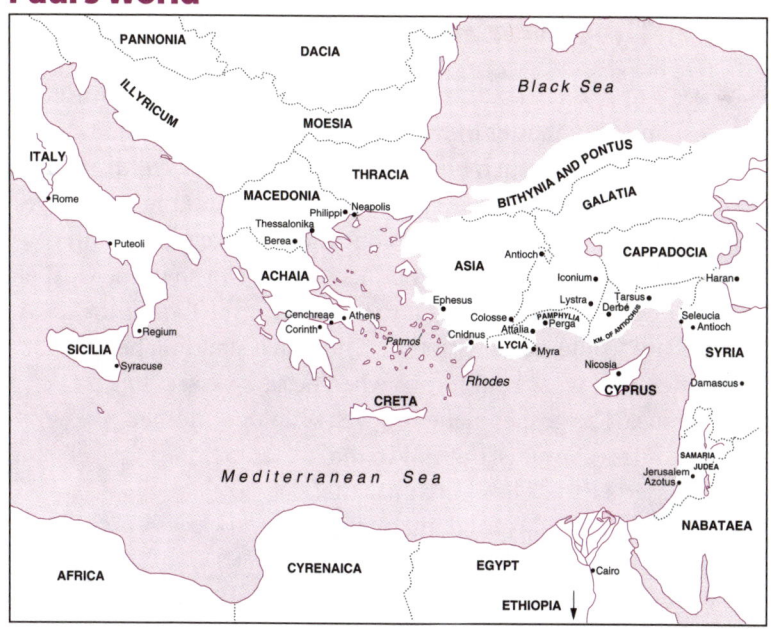

are under a curse" (Galatians 3:10 NIV). He is not worried about whom he insults or aggravates. He even dares to disagree with Peter (Galatians 2:14) on matters of church fellowship. Paul is clear on one point only: Christ has abolished Jewish law. And the urgent tone of the letter to the Galatians makes it clear that if this point doesn't get through to them, Paul is afraid the congregation will abandon the gospel.

> **Paul's conflict** with Peter was over the relationship of the Law to the Gentile mission. One such example was over circumcision (Galatians 2).

Paul is completely focused on the one thing that has turned his life around and made him into a human megaphone for the church—the risen Christ. No one but God can take a life and turn it around 180 degrees so that we all have to sit up, take notice, and say with Paul, "And they praised God because of me" (Galatians 1:24 NIV).

> **Paul does not like** angels because they were used in Hebrew tradition to mediate the law (Galatians 3:19).

Paul's Boldness in Preaching

1 Corinthians 1:18-25; 2:1-5
Christ: The Power and Wisdom of God

IN GREEK AND HELLENISTIC CULTURE, making a mistake was merely a matter of bad aim. For the Greeks, wisdom was a way of avoiding such mistakes. Heroes in Greek culture were both born and raised. A male child had to have the advantages of breeding and a closely tutored education to take full advantage of the legal rights and privileges of his society. Not so in the Gospel, says Paul. Someone has said that the ground at the foot of the cross is level. Paul would agree with that. This equal standing before God is the essence of what Paul means when he says we are "one in Christ Jesus." The gospel makes us even with one another.

Foolishness abounds, but not in the church, asserts Paul. The church has the Word, and that Word is fundamentally opposed to the wisdom of the world. In fact, God's foolishness in the crucified Messiah dares to stand in stark contrast to all of the wisdom of the ages handed down from Egypt, Mesopotamia, Greece, and Rome. The wisdom of Christ is foolishness in the eyes of the world because it all hinges on a man who hung on a cross.

> **Because Corinth** was an important trading center in Greece, it was home to many different philosophies and ideas. Moral corruption was rampant in Corinth.

God chose to shut the eyes of the worldly wise and to reveal his Gospel to the foolish. This brings us directly to the core of the matter: God's power is not recognized by the world. God's grace and wisdom are revealed "to those whom God has called" (1 Corinthians 1:24 NIV).

God's "foolishness" in Christ once again turns everything on its head because not only is God's wisdom revealed to those who are called, but God does so to "shame" the wise and the strong (1 Corinthians 1:27).

Why should God want to shame the world and its wisdom? Paul says that God will "nullify the things that are...so that no one may boast before him" (1 Corinthians 1:28-29 NIV). It seems that Paul is not going to let anyone go away half-hearted when

(Continued on page 27)

HOW THE BIBLE IS ORGANIZED

The Bible is divided into two "testaments." The Old Testament, which was originally written in Hebrew, contains four major sections that include 39 individual books. The New Testament, which was originally written in Greek, is divided into three sections that include 27 books.

THE OLD TESTAMENT

The Pentateuch
- Genesis
- Exodus
- Leviticus
- Numbers
- Deuteronomy

History
- Joshua
- Judges
- Ruth
- 1 and 2 Samuel
- 1 and 2 Kings
- 1 and 2 Chronicles
- Ezra
- Nehemiah
- Esther

Wisdom
- Job
- Psalms
- Proverbs
- Ecclesiastes
- Song of Solomon

Prophets
- Isaiah
- Jeremiah
- Lamentations
- Ezekiel
- Daniel
- Hosea
- Joel
- Amos
- Obadiah
- Jonah
- Micah
- Nahum
- Habakkuk
- Zephaniah
- Haggai
- Zechariah
- Malachi

THE NEW TESTAMENT

The Gospels
- Matthew
- Mark
- Luke
- John

History
- Acts of the Apostles

The Letters
- Romans
- 1 and 2 Corinthians
- Galatians
- Ephesians
- Philippians
- Colossians
- 1 and 2 Thessalonians
- 1 and 2 Timothy
- Titus
- Philemon
- Hebrews
- James
- 1 and 2 Peter
- 1, 2, and 3 John
- Jude
- Revelation

Adapted from *A Beginner's Guide to Reading the Bible* by Craig R. Koester, copyright © 1991 Augsburg Fortress.

BIBLE TIME LINE

Date	Bible Story/Message	Text
	Creation	Genesis 1:1—2:4a
	The Fall	Genesis 3:1-24
	The Flood	Gen. 6:11-22; 9:8-17
	Call of Abraham	Genesis 12:1-3
	Abraham and Sarah	Genesis 18:1-15
	Moses	Exodus 3:1-15
1275-1235 B.C.	**Exodus and Wilderness Wandering**	
	Wilderness Wandering	Exodus 16:1-12
	The Ten Commandments	Exodus 20:1-17
	The Shema	Deuteronomy 6:4-9
1200-1050 B.C.	**Judges**	
	Deborah and Barak	Judges 4:1-24
	Ruth and Naomi	Ruth 1:1-18
1050-922 B.C.	**United Monarchy**	
	David	2 Samuel 7:1-29
	The Divine Shepherd	Psalm 23:1-6
	Thanks for Healing	Psalm 30:4-5
922-721 B.C.	**Divided Monarchy**	
	Micah	Micah 6:8
	Jeremiah	Jeremiah 1:4-19
	The Fiery Furnace	Daniel 3:1-30
	Fall of Northern Kingdom	2 Kings 17:5-23
586-538 B.C.	**Judah in Exile**	
538-333 B.C.	**Persian Period**	
333-165 B.C.	**Hellenistic Period**	
165-63 B.C.	**Maccabean Period**	
63 B.C.-A.D. 637	**Roman Period**	
	Mary	Luke 1:26-38

24　Ten Key Teachings from Paul's Letters

Date	Bible Story/Message	Text
4 B.C.	**Jesus is Born**	
	Birth of Jesus	Luke 2:1-20
	Birth of Jesus	Matthew 1:1, 17-25
	Baptism of Jesus	Matthew 3:13-17
	Temptation of Jesus	Luke 4:1-13
A.D. 20	**Ministry of Jesus**	
	Sermon on the Mount	Matthew 7:1-12
	Healing a Paralytic	Mark 2:1-12
	The Gospel in Miniature	John 3:16
	Cleansing the Temple	Mark 11:15-19
	Mary and Martha	Luke 10:38-42
	Peter	Matthew 16:13-23
	The Lord's Supper	Matthew 26:17-30
	I Am the Way	John 14:6
	The Crucifixion	Mark 15:21-39
	The Death of Jesus	John 19:1-30
	The Road to Emmaus	Luke 24:13-35
	Jesus' Resurrection	John 20:1-18
	The Ascension of Jesus	Acts 1:6-11
	Pentecost	Acts 2:1-14, 37-42
A.D. 40	**Apostles' Ministry**	
	Paul	Acts 9:1-22
	Benediction	2 Thess. 2:16-17
	A New Creation	2 Cor. 5:17-21
	God's Love in Christ Jesus	Romans 8:31-39
	By Grace	Ephesians 2:8-10
	Faith	Hebrews 11:1-3
	Encouragement and Warnings	Hebrews 12:1-2
	The Alpha and Omega	Revelation 1:8

Bible Time Line

HOW TO READ THE BIBLE

Finding a Bible Reference
1. Check the Bible's table of contents if you do not know where the book is.
2. In your Bible, the chapter numbers are large numbers, usually at the beginning of paragraphs. The chapter numbers might be also printed at the top of each page.
3. The verse numbers are tiny numbers, usually printed at the beginning of sentences.

> **Psalm 119:105**
> book of the Bible — chapter — verse

Understanding What You Read
As you read a passage of the Bible, keep in mind these three questions:
1. What does this text tell me about God?
2. What does this text tell me about the people of God?
3. What does this text tell me about myself?

Going Deeper
Other questions that might help you understand what you are reading include:
1. What type of literature is this passage? Is it a story? A historical account? Poetry? A hymn? A letter? How might that affect my understanding of the passage?
2. What is the historical situation of the writer?
3. Who is speaking in this passage?
4. Who is being addressed in this passage? How am I like or different from that person or group?
5. How does the passage relate to the surrounding text? Does the surrounding material shed any light on the passage's meaning?
6. What are the key words and phrases in the passage? Which ones do I not understand?
7. How does the passage compare to parallel passages or to texts on the same subject?
8. What in the passage puzzles, surprises, or confuses me?

Marking Your Bible
When you read the Bible, make notes to yourself about questions and insights you have as you read. The following symbols might be helpful.

- ㉓   The circled number marks an important chapter.
- ?   I do not understand this.
- ♥   God's love is revealed in this passage.
- P   One of God's promises is given here.
- †   This is about something God has done for me.
- HS   The work of the Holy Spirit is described here.
- F   Faith, confidence, trust
- H   Hope, perseverance, patience
- ↔   Love, relationships, social concerns
- ℘   Prayer
- ♪   Praise, joy, hymns
- ℞   Strength, comfort, healing

"Going Deeper" and "Marking Your Bible" are adapted from *Bible Reading Handbook* by Paul Schuessler, copyright © 1991 Augsburg Fortress.

Ten Key Teachings from Paul's Letters

(Continued from page 22)

it comes to the Gospel. Those who are being saved and those who are perishing will most certainly know why. They will have to look at the crucified Christ—God's foolishness—squarely in the face before claiming any wisdom for themselves. All this, says Paul, so that we will not boast but are driven to despair about our own wisdom, power, and ability to save ourselves. All this, says Paul, so that we are led finally, gently, and by the hand of loving Lord to claim Christ's righteousness for ourselves (1 Corinthians 1:30). All this so that we don't perish but are saved.

Paul's message for us here is that God's power alone is at work in this proclamation. He speaks plainly because he believes it is a matter of life and death for the church and for every believer. For Paul, to perish at the hands of the world is nothing compared to perishing and not knowing Christ. All the wisdom in the world will not hold a candle to one gram of faith in Christ.

> ***Ecclesia*** is the Greek word Paul uses for the church. It's a secular term from Greek democracy meaning "assembly."

Enmeshed in Paul's letter to the Galatians is the fact of a changed life. Once the law was a disciplinarian (custodian RSV), but since Christ that external control is no longer necessary. Once salvation was dependent upon works of the law. Now justification is by Christ. Once we were enslaved to the spirits of the world but now we are redeemed. Once we were slaves. Now we are free. The list goes on and on, enumerating the changes that have become part of the Christian's life. "For freedom," Paul writes, "Christ has set us free. Stand firm, therefore, and do not submit again to a yoke of slavery (Galatians 5:1).

Focus the Stories

Life and Death

Paul says, "I died to the law, so that I might live to God. I have been crucified with Christ; and it is no longer I who live, but it is Christ who lives in me" (Galatians 2:19-20a). What do you think Paul meant by these words? How would you describe the Christ who lives in you? How would you describe the Christ who loves in you?

Wisdom

Think about how we determine what is wise and what is not. What are the conditions for intelligent decisions? What is the difference between intelligence and wisdom? Can you describe someone who you would consider to be a "wise" person? What are the characteristics of that person? How does "common sense" play into any definition of wisdom?

Revelation

Paul makes a strong case in Galatians 3:28 to minimize our differences and then concludes that we are "one in Christ." How does that make you feel? How important is it for us to minimize our differences?

Power

Think about the ways in which power is portrayed in our society. What are the symbols of power? How do we know when someone is powerful or not? When might weakness be considered a sign of strength? What do you think of the saying that "a hero is only as great as his/her heart?" Does this have any bearing on our understanding of what power is today? How would you define the power of God? Where do you see evidence of it? How do you see that power manifested in your life?

Experience

Someone has said that an experience should never be at the mercy of an argument. Paul's conversion experience on the road to Damascus (Acts 9:1-19) fortified Paul's ministry in reassuring him of his convictions in the gospel. What experiences in your life can you recall that have fortified your faith and reassured you in your beliefs? Have there been other experiences in your life that have affected your faith?

Closing

Paul's emphasis as seen in Session 3 centers on the truth of the Gospel as Paul preached it, as well as Paul's authority to preach. Paul's concern is that the Gospel not become blurred or dimmed, but that the centrality of Christ be paramount. Paul recognizes that the message of Christ might look like foolishness to the rest of the world, but to the church the message of the Gospel should be unmistakable.

Closing prayer: Almighty God, grant that we, who have been redeemed from the old life of sin by our baptism into the death and resurrection of your Son Jesus Christ, may be renewed in your Holy Spirit to live in righteousness and true holiness; through Jesus Christ our Lord. Amen.

4 The Freedom of the Christian

Free indeed! We are free indeed!

Romans 8:1-4   Life in the Spirit

BEFORE SAYING there is now "no condemnation for those who are in Christ Jesus," Paul took a great deal of trouble to be clear about the nature of sin and how impossible it is to separate oneself from the impulses and desires of the flesh. It is the nature of sin to avoid looking too closely for fear of what it might find. Paul concedes that reason (the mind) is capable of imagining something different—that is, God's law—but that the flesh can't comply. "I do not understand my own actions. For I do not do what I want, but I do the very thing I hate" (Romans 7:15). If it were a court of law, we would be condemned on the basis of our inability to do the good that we intend to do.

If there is no condemnation for those who are in Christ Jesus, it is because a price has been paid that satisfied the demands of the law. Another law, the "law of the spirit," now operates in place of the old law of death. We are free because of the righteousness of Jesus Christ, who died for us and claimed the victory over death for us.

There is a reference to a "sin offering" that goes back

> *For sin will have no dominion over you, since you are not under law but under grace.*
>
> Romans 6:14

The Freedom of the Christian   31

> **The core** of Paul's understanding of the gospel is Romans 5–8. Here is the essence of Paul's theology.

to the law of Israel. In the old law or covenant, a burnt offering or grain offering had to be given to atone for the transgressions of anyone. In the book of Job, we learn of the reveling and partying of Job's children and Job's concern about their behavior. Thinking, "It may be that my children have sinned, and cursed God in their hearts" (Job 1:5), Job makes an atonement for his son's parties with a burnt offering the day after. An in-kind offering had to be made according to the level of the transgression. That was the "old" law.

The "new law" in Christ holds true in many ways to the standard for the old but the difference is that Christ is the "sin offering" once and for all. Paul again emphasizes that Christ does not come to overturn the old order of things, but comes to re-establish the old in terms of the new. Christ comes to infuse the old order with new life, new direction, new beginnings. He makes old wine into new wine, old laws of retribution into a new "law" of grace, and old divisions and sorrows are wiped away. The language of the prophet Isaiah comes as close as possible to expressing what Christ does when he says there will be water in the desert and new highways will spring up (Isaiah 35:6-8).

The fulfillment of the old law by Christ for our sake is sometimes difficult for us to accept. We succumb to a "It's too good to be true" mentality and thereby deny the goodness of God. Really, what we are doing in such circumstances is reducing God to a level of humanity. The love God has for each of us far surpasses any level of human love, so much so that faith is required in order for our ability to believe it.

We live in a world that seems willing to forgive some things and not others, that overlooks some things and not others, that forgets some things and not others. The Christian is accountable to the world for

> **Martin Luther** summarized the purpose of the law in three respects: (1) The law is an aid to order in the world; (2) The law is like a mirror showing us our sins; (3) The law teaches us how to lead a God-pleasing life. Jesus said, "Do not think that I have come to abolish the law or the prophets; I have come not to abolish but to fulfill" (Matthew 5:17).

> **For I am convinced that neither death, nor life, nor angels, nor rulers, nor things present, nor things to come, nor powers, nor height, nor depth, nor anything else in all creation, will be able to separate us from the love of God in Christ Jesus our Lord.**
>
> Romans 8:38-39

infractions committed, but where God is concerned, we have fulfilled the new law through our faith in Jesus as our Savior. That is the freedom of the Christian. We have been set free from anxiety about "being good enough."

God does not abolish the old law with the coming of Christ, says Paul, but the old law becomes "powerless" to do what it needs to do because it is based on sin and has to do with regulating sin in the community. The focus for the Christian community is no longer prevention and regulation of sin but freedom in Christ. This means that the focus of our lives should not be on sinning or not sinning but on Christ. God has made sure that if we believe in Jesus and are baptized into the community of Christ, we will be considered "fully righteous" in God's eyes (i.e., "in order that the righteous requirements of the law might be fully met in us," Romans 8:4 NIV). That is because God now looks at us through the eyeglasses of the cross. God no longer sees us for who we are, but sees us through the price paid for us on the cross by God's Son.

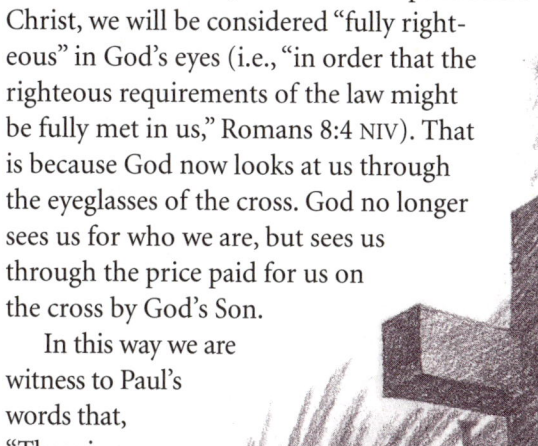

In this way we are witness to Paul's words that, "There is now no condemnation for those who are in Christ Jesus" (Romans 8:1 NIV).

The Freedom of the Christian

Galatians 5:13-14 Christian Freedom

WE ARE SO FAMILIAR with the passage, "Love your neighbor as yourself," that we tend to be a bit skeptical about what it means for us today. Since we are free in Christ, Paul encourages us to exercise that freedom by becoming slaves to one another in loving ways. Paul is reminding the church that we have been given a different calling than the world at large. We are to love our neighbors as ourselves. We love our neighbors because we need to love. God has so loved us that our spirit overflows in love to our neighbor. God has so showered us with riches that it instills in us the need to give. God has forgiven us so often that we can do no less than forgive our brother or sister who sins against us. Not out of a sense of law do we love our neighbors, but as a loving response to the love we've received in Christ Jesus.

> *Therefore, I tell you, her sins, which were many, have been forgiven; hence she has shown great love. But the one to whom little is forgiven, loves little.*
> Luke 7:47

What does Paul mean when he warns about indulging our "sinful nature?" The classic seven deadly sins are a short list of what Paul could be talking about when he refers to indulging our sinful nature: pride, lust, greed, sloth, gluttony, jealousy, and anger. Our sinful nature is all too obvious.

Immorality in the city of Corinth was so prevalent that people would sew small bells in their clothes to signal another person if there was a sexual interest.

Paul does not ask the Christian community to exist as a utopia on earth. There will be problems in the church. There will be hypocrisy, jealousy, pride, lust for power, and all of the other things that we encounter in communities outside of the church. Paul is simply saying here that we cannot use our new freedom in Christ as an excuse or a reason to

The seven deadly sins (pride, greed, sloth, gluttony, envy, anger, and lust) are represented in many medieval woodcuts.

continue to be divisive and power-hungry within the church. Paul's love for the church causes him to be realistic about what can happen in any community. He knows that if Christian people let their own emotions and their need to feel powerful take over, they will be destroyed by each other.

> **Love is patient; love is kind; love is not envious or boastful or arrogant or rude. It does not insist on its own way; it is not irritable or resentful; it does not rejoice in wrongdoing, but rejoices in the truth. It bears all things, believes all things, hopes all things, endures all things. Love never ends.**
>
> 1 Corinthians 13:4-8a

"Love your neighbor as yourself." This statement makes all kinds of sense in the modern psychological sense. If we can't love ourselves, to what extent can we love anyone else? We are encouraged not to be dependent or co-dependent on other people in order to determine our identity. Christ tells us who we are. We are dependent upon Christ for the new and true sense of who we are. Christ has determined our value. To whatever extent we can own the identity of being loved and forgiven by Christ, then we can love our neighbor as we do ourselves.

If we try to love others in a selfless way, we usually fail. Usually we have selfish motives and want something in return. Jesus shows us what it means to be selfless in our love for other people without expecting any reward at all.

Loving others is difficult, for many times our love will not be understood as love. Sometimes not giving someone what he or she wants is love. Parents must occasionally say "no," and they do it out of love. Because Christ's love often stands in contrast to how the world defines love, misunderstandings can occur.

Because God has loved us to such a great and extreme sense, those seeds of love will produce an abundance of loving acts toward the neighbor we know as well

> **Three places** in the scriptures where God says, "I love you" are Isaiah 43:2; Jeremiah 31:3; and John 15:9.

The Freedom of the Christian

as the neighbor we don't know. Anything we are able to do for our neighbor is done because Christ has already done all there is to do for us.

The community in Christ is called to freedom and to love. We are free to serve one another in love.

Focus the Stories

Freedom From and Freedom For

When someone offends or wrongs us, our temptation might be to retaliate in a like manner. Christ has made it possible for us to be free from responding to others in attitudes of retaliation and revenge. Instead, we are free to respond in love to others even when their behavior may not warrant that love. How does such an attitude set us free?

Newness in Christ

What comes to mind when you think of something new? Can you picture yourself as new? In what ways? Think about ways in which Christ makes everything new. What does it mean to be made new? What does it mean that we can be reborn? What are the implications of this?

Serving One Another in Love

Reflect on ways to serve others. How can we serve others in whatever settings we find ourselves (job, school, home)? How is the example of Mother Teresa appropriate here? What is the difference in serving because one is saved rather than serving in order to be saved? Which of those two choices most closely reflects Paul's thinking? How does serving in love differ from being self-serving?

Sin

Lutherans have many ways of confessing their sins in worship. One earlier Lutheran confession stated, "We are by nature, sinful and unclean... ." A contemporary confession states, "We are in bondage to sin and cannot free ourselves... ." How are these two confessions different? How are they the same? Do you have a preference for one? If so, why? Is sin quantifiable? If the act is sinful (such as stealing) can it be justified if the motive is commendable (for example, to feed a starving child)?

Closing

Session 4 concerned itself with a "before and after" situation. Before Christ, any sin had to be compensated for by some act of atonement. Jesus became the atonement for all our sins, and that pivotal moment in history divided the before and after. Living in the "after" as we do, we recognize a tremendous freedom that gives us a peace the world cannot understand. Through Christ, we have been made new, which creates faithful and loving people. We have been set free.

Closing prayer: Gracious God, you have released us from the restraints of the old law. You have taken away the penalty of our sin and placed it on yourself. Our thanks to you is born in our hearts and grows in our love to others. Instill in us the desire to radiate love to all we meet, and continue to bless us that we might reflect you who set us free to our neighbor. Amen.

5 God as Provider

The presence of God in comfort and promise.

2 Corinthians 1:3-4 God's Comfort

GOD IS A COMFORTER, the source of our comfort in any kind of affliction. Like a parent comforts a child, God's nature is to comfort us when we are sorrowful, and the marvel of it all is that God does not comfort us with the reserve of some bystander, but enters into our pain. When we hurt, God hurts. God is often portrayed in the scriptures as a shepherd. The people of Biblical times understood a shepherd's love. A shepherd knew every animal in his flock. He would call them by name. The shepherd would put his life on the line for the sake of his flock. He would do everything in his power to care for them. When they were sick or injured, he carried them. God is our shepherd. God cares for us, keeps us, takes us by the hand as well as comforts us. So determined to care for us, God sent both Jesus and the Holy Spirit to comfort and console us.

> **When he saw the crowds, he had compassion for them, because they were harassed and helpless, like sheep without a shepherd.**
> Matthew 9:36

God sends the Holy Spirit, the Comforter, to speak in our behalf "with sighs too deep for words," writes Paul (Romans 8:26). The Holy Spirit is an intangible presence that can bring peace to a troubled heart. Whatever the cause of our pain and sorrow, the Holy Spirit comforts us with a peace that "surpasses all understanding,"

> **Our word** *compassion* comes from a Greek word meaning "bowels." Compassion is a gut feeling resonating from deep within us.

Paul wrote to the Philippians (4:7). The Holy Spirit, our gift in baptism, accompanies us throughout our lives, counseling, comforting, and consoling us in all our afflictions. We are never alone. Never abandoned. Never left to cope on our own. Instead the Holy Spirit can be God's hand that takes us and walks with us through each day as well as every valley. The Holy Spirit is one way God "keeps us."

We are also comforted through God's Son, Jesus, who has paid the penalty for our sins and now offers us full pardon and forgiveness. So, if our afflictions and troubles are the result of our own sinfulness, God still desires to comfort us by forgiving us our sins.

> *I am the LORD, I have called you in righteousness, I have taken you by the hand and kept you.*
>
> Isaiah 42:6a

The apostle John writes that God is love and then goes on to say that God revealed that deep love for us by sending Jesus, the beloved son, to be the atoning sacrifice for our sins (1 John 4:8-10). Such a love is probably too deep, too profound that it defies our understanding. Then consider the love of Jesus for us as he suffered persecution, pain, ostracism, and an agonizing death so that we might be forgiven of our sins. No sin is too great to separate us from the love of Christ (Romans 8:39). That should be an incredible comfort to us all.

Finally, God provides the church, the assembly of believers, to offer comfort and consolation to us when we are hurting. Of course anyone can offer another consolation, but often the most meaningful consolation and comfort is from someone who has "been there, done that." Their experiences in sorrow give them an authority to console another that has no equal.

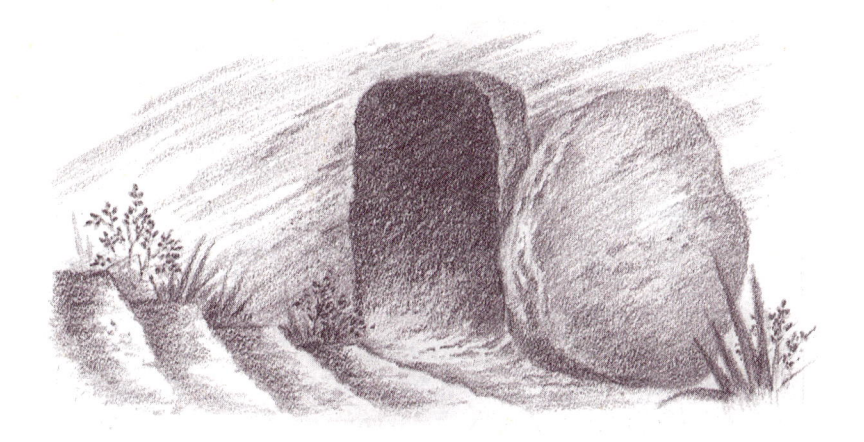

Extending comfort and consolation in healing words of love and forgiveness as well as acts of kindness become our privilege. To be invited into the inner circle of another's pain is a rich reward. It is to be blessed. Blessed to be a blessing.

Paul does not make distinctions between big troubles and little ones. Trouble comes in all sizes. It comes when we aren't looking for it, and it comes at any time despite our best intentions. When we pass on to others the comfort we have received from Christ, we reassure our neighbors of their importance and that God cares about them in their afflictions.

> **Paul the Apostle** called to the Gentiles (Romans 11:13-14). Paul decides in Acts 18:6 that he will preach only to the Gentiles.

So consolation and comfort come full circle. God comforts us that we might comfort others. So it is with God, who always gives to us before expecting anything in return. Our response to God's comfort is thanksgiving and an offering of comfort and consolation to our neighbor in their pain and sorrow.

God as Provider

Romans 1:1-4 God's Promise

PAUL REMINDS US in this passage that Jesus is the heir to the Hebrew tradition preached by the prophets in the Old Testament. The Jewish tradition preached the coming of a mighty warrior and king who is called "Messiah" and who would conquer the Jewish oppressors. But Paul's assertion that Jesus is the descendant of David, who was "declared with power to be the Son of God," is a bold and courageous claim. The Messiah that Paul preaches is not the kind of warrior king that the people of Israel expected. Instead, Paul's Messiah came in suffering to forgive the sins of the world.

> **Paul's letters** are not arranged in the scriptures chronologically but by length, Romans being the longest and, consequently, the first.

Paul relies on the promises of God in the same way the Israelites relied on those promises. God had promised Israel land, freedom from exile, a Messiah, and future generations. Most of all, God promised Israel an abiding presence. After all, they were God's chosen people. They are still God's chosen people, but today Christians alike can claim that status as well. In Romans 11, Paul likens our inclusion as chosen people as a branch grafted onto a tree, and in Galatians 4, Paul uses the metaphor of adoption to indicate our status as chosen people of God.

> *For a child has been born for us, a son given to us; authority rests upon his shoulders; and he is named Wonderful Counselor, Mighty God, Everlasting Father, Prince of Peace.*
> Isaiah 9:6

That Jesus is the Christ is news on which Paul stakes his reputation. Paul puts everything he has done and will do on the line for this one message: Jesus Christ is the Messiah and the Son of God, our Lord.

Nowhere in the New Testament does Jesus ever call himself the Son of God. This claim is made by others—the disciples, a blind man, a leper, a dove from heaven, and a soldier at the crucifixion. Paul's confidence regarding the Messiahship of Jesus of Nazareth as the Son of God and the risen Christ is the most compelling witness that we have in the New Testament.

No other scriptural writer comes as close to making the case for Jesus as the Son of God as does Paul. Yet Paul never knew Jesus in person. Paul's claim of Jesus as Messiah is double-edged, because it relies on the human tradition (Israel) and the promise of the Holy Spirit (God). The claim is that Jesus is both God and man. Not just one or the other, but both in the form of crucified and resurrected Lord. Many people have trouble with this concept because it is difficult to imagine that any person could be fully human and fully divine at the same time. But if we think about it, many things have multiple facets. Many fruits have peelings, a flesh, and a core all in one. A tree has roots, trunk, branches, leaves, and often seeds all in one. As people we are physical, emotional, intellectual, and spiritual beings, so perhaps being fully divine and fully human simultaneously might not be such an unimaginable thing. Again, God's promise is the key to understanding this mystery.

If this Jesus "who was declared with power to be the Son of God by his resurrection from the dead" (Romans 1:4 NIV) is not the cornerstone of the church, then all is lost. As Christians we look to this promise, to this Word, and rely on it and draw our comfort and strength from it. Our hope rests in this promise, and so does our future. Paul gives us hope that we can last through the storms and trouble of our lives with this one promise alone, and testifies to the power of God to make it so for us.

> *Since, then, we have a great high priest who has passed through the heavens, Jesus, the Son of God, let us hold fast to our confession. For we do not have a high priest who is unable to sympathize with our weaknesses, but we have one who in every respect has been tested as we are, yet without sin. Let us therefore approach the throne of grace with boldness, so that we may receive mercy and find grace to help in time of need.*
> Hebrews 4:14-16

Focus the Stories

Luke 2:29-32 NIV *(Song of Simeon)*

"Sovereign Lord, as you have promised,
  you now dismiss your servant in peace.
For my eyes have seen your salvation,
  which you have prepared in the sight of all people,
a light for revelation to the Gentiles
  and for glory to your people Israel."

1. How might this passage, originally from Isaiah 9:2, 6-7, be seen as prophecy of Jesus as the Messiah? Why do you think the Jewish people discounted these verses as any indication of Jesus as Messiah? What difference does it make in our daily lives that we see Jesus as the subject of this prophecy?

2. Recall a time when you were comforted or consoled. How do you see God working in the situation?

3. God gives to us before asking us to give anything in return. What, then, is the reason that in some worship services, the offering is often received after God's word is proclaimed? What does such a practice say about the nature of God as well as our understanding of worship?

4. Try to list all of the promises God has made in the Bible that you can think of in preparation for the group discussion.

5. Complete the following sentence: "When I trust the promises of God, I…".

6. Describe ways you could comfort or console another person.

Closing

Session 5 presents a challenge. Since we have been made new in Christ, or to say it another way, since Christ has set us free from the power of sin, we are free to love one another. Paul wants the church to be an experience in love. Recognizing there will be problems, Paul urges the church to act in Christlike fashion and love our neighbor as ourselves. God is a comforter through the Holy Spirit, Jesus, and the church. We finished our study by noting Paul's emphasis of God's promise both to accompany us as well as to save us. It is a promise we can count on.

Closing prayer: Gracious God, we stand in awe of the depths of your love for us. While we are as but a speck of dust in all creation, a millisecond of time in your age, you have stooped to save us. Let your love so fill us that we might love those both near and far. Give us your peace that we might dwell securely in the certainty of our salvation. In the name of Jesus Christ, our Savior, we pray. Amen.

6 Rejoice in the Lord Always

May the peace of Christ guard your heart and mind.

Philippians 4:4-7   No Need for Anxiety

CHRIST IS IN OUR MIDST! Our sinful nature has been swept clean and made pure and righteous by Christ's death and resurrection. Nothing we can do or will do can keep God's love from us. Therefore, we are free to fill our days with rejoicing and thanksgiving, because Christ has already attained salvation for us. God's peace is a gift, an ordinary, everyday reality that works in our midst through the Holy Spirit to sanctify and transform the church.

Paul's parting words to one of his favorite congregations, the Philippians, are a series of gentle imperatives. The repeated command, "Rejoice," can also be interpreted as a farewell, so it is unclear how this word is to be interpreted. What is clear is Paul's urging the people to display a sense of gentleness.

Gentleness is a quality born out of a sense of well-being. In this letter of joy Paul tells the congregation that he thanks God every time he remembers them (Philippians 1:3). Then Paul closes his letter with some parental advice.

"Don't worry about anything," Paul admonishes. Just let God know your requests, adding that it can be done in an attitude of thanksgiving. Paul assures his people that everything will be all right. To put a capstone on that assurance, Paul poetically proclaims that a peace from God so incredible it defies understanding will guard both their hearts and their minds.

When the temptation to worry about the future comes to us, we can let our prayer requests be known to God and then be comforted in a peace that goes beyond our ability to comprehend the guarding of our entire being.

It is not necessary to comprehend all we have studied. Rather, it is quite enough to believe that Jesus replaced the old law of atonement with a new covenant of grace. It is in that umbrella of grace that we reside, comforted by a God who guards our entire being with a peace that exceeds our understanding.

> *Rejoice in the Lord always; again I will say, Rejoice. Let your gentleness be known to everyone. The Lord is near. Do not worry about anything, but in everything by prayer and supplication with thanksgiving let your requests be made known to God. And the peace of God, which surpasses all understanding, will guard your hearts and your minds in Christ Jesus.*
>
> Philippians 4:4-7

Focus the Story

1. How can we make all our requests known to God and not reduce God to some spiritual "Santa Claus?" Is there a reason Paul would write these words, and what do you think that might be? How does Paul view our relationship to God? How would you describe your relationship to God?

2. Paul writes that the Lord is near. How close is the Lord to you? On what do you base that assurance? If you feel as if the Lord is not close to you, how might you change that?

3. What are some questions this study has brought to mind for you? Have they been answered? If not, what would be good places in which to find those answers? What areas of Paul's teachings or aspects of his thinking remain as questions or concerns for you?

4. For you, what has been the most significant aspect of this study?

5. How would you define the "peace of God?" How does it differ from other concepts and definitions of peace?

Closing

The peace of Christ is a spiritual presence that far surpasses any earthly peace. The peace of Christ is a spiritual gift that is ours if we so desire it, yet it takes some discipline on our part to make that gift work for us. Faith, too, is a gift, but its growth depends on how well we nourish it, as does that peace of Christ.

Closing prayer: Almighty God, giver of all things, with gladness we give thanks for all your goodness. We bless you for the love which has created and which sustains us from day to day. We praise you for the gift of your Son our Savior, through whom you have made known your will and grace. We thank you for the Holy Spirit, the comforter; for your holy Church; for the means of grace; for the lives of all faithful and good people; and for the hope of the life to come. Help us to treasure in our hearts all that our Lord has done for us, and enable us to show our thankfulness by lives that are wholly given to your service.